D0996246

Clothes and Costume

Jane Shuter

Illustrated by Mark Bergin, James Field, John James

HISTORY OF BRITAIN – CLOTHES AND COSTUME
was produced for Heinemann Children's Reference
by Lionheart Books, London.

Editor: Lionel Bender
Designer: Ben White
Editorial Assistant: Madeleine Samuel
Picture Researcher: Jennie Karrach
Media Conversion and Typesetting: Peter MacDonald
        & Michael Weintroub
Editorial Advisors: Andrew Farrow, Paul Shuter

Production Controller: Lorraine Stebbing
Editorial Director: David Riley

First published in Great Britain in 1997 by
Heinemann Educational Publishers, a division of Reed
Educational and Professional Publishing Limited,
Halley Court, Jordan Hill, Oxford OX2 8EJ.

MADRID ATHENS
FLORENCE PRAGUE WARSAW
PORTSMOUTH NH CHICAGO SAO PAULO MEXICO
SINGAPORE TOKYO MELBOURNE AUCKLAND
IBADAN GABORONE JOHANNESBURG KAMPALA NAIROBI

ISBN 0431 05724 9 Hb   ISBN 0431 05733 8 Pb

British Library Cataloguing-in-Publication Data.
A catalogue record for this book is available
from the British Library.

Printed in Hong Kong by Wing King Tong Company Limited

Acknowledgements
Picture credits
Pages 4: C. M. Dixon. 5: C. M. Dixon. 6: Michael Holford.
7: Michael Holford. 8-9: The British Library/Cott. Claud B IV
f24v 8450531. 11 left: The Fotomas Index. 11 right:
Michael Holford. 12-13: Michael Holford. 13: The
Archbishop of Canterbury and the Trustees of Lambeth
Palace Library. 15: The British Library/ADD 42130,
166v,7950562. 17: The British Library, London.
19 top: The Fotomas Index. 19 bottom: National Trust
Photographic Library/Derrick E. Witty. 20: The Bridgeman
Art Library/The British Library. Roy 15 Elll f.102. 21: The
Fotomas Index. 22-23: The Bridgeman Art Library/Private
Collection. 23 top: The Radio Times Hulton Picture
Library/Corbis Photos. 24: Fine Art Photographic Library
Ltd. 25: Hulton Deutsch/Corbis Photos. 26: The Bridgeman
Art Library/Royal Holloway and Bedford New College,
Surrey. 27, 28-29: Hulton Deutsch/Corbis Photos. 29:
Zefa.

Artwork credits
Main illustrators: Mark Bergin, John James, James Field.
Additional illustrations by Bill Donohoe.

Cover: Artwork by John James

INTRODUCTION

Throughout history, people have worn a variety of clothes, cut their hair in different ways, and put on make-up and jewellery. Their clothes and body ornaments can tell us a great deal about what it was like to live at the time – how they made their own cloth, for example. They can reveal whether people were rich enough to buy these things from other people or had to make their own. They can indicate whether people wore special clothes for different jobs – were there clothes that only rich and important people wore? Looking at what people wore gives us a fascinating insight into the changing face of Britain over the centuries.

CONTENTS

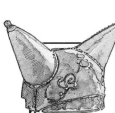

EARLY PEOPLE

In 54 BC, Julius Caesar, the Roman general, wrote this of the British: "In Kent and along the coast they are most civilized. Further inland they wear nothing but animal skins. All Britons paint themselves with woad, wear their hair long and shave their bodies, except the top lip."

He was talking about the men. He saw the British as barbarians, and took no notice of their women at all. Clearly, the most basic sort of clothing in early Britain was animal skins. Caesar's 'more civilized' Britons wore clothes made from woven cloth. They spun, dyed and wove each piece of cloth by hand.

△ **Cloth was woven on a wooden loom.** The piece of cloth shown here would have taken three weeks to weave.

▽ **Detail from a Celtic bronze cauldron showing a man wearing a torc.** The cauldron dates from about 200 BC. Torcs were neck rings worn by important people as a symbol of their wealth. Some Celtic warriors fought wearing little else!

▷ **This man's magnificent shield, metal armour and sword and the woman's gold bracelets** show they are an important couple. Maybe the man is a leader of one of the tribes that lived in Britain before the Romans invaded.

British cloth was made from wool that was spun then coloured with plant dyes. Various vegetables, leaves and flowers, when boiled, make a weak dye. The coloured wools were woven into striped and checked cloth. The colours – mostly reds, greens and browns – did not stay bright for long as the dyes soon washed out of the cloth.

Clothing designs were simple. Everyone – young and old, rich and poor – wore the same styles. Women wore long tunic dresses, and men wore tunics and trousers tied at the ankles. They wore cloaks, not coats. Wool was hard-wearing, so people wore the same clothes, well mended, for years.

▷ **A group of Britons** that Caesar would have said were "well dressed". They are probably merchants who traded with Celts in Gaul so can afford good clothes. They wear plain, almost shapeless, leather shoes.

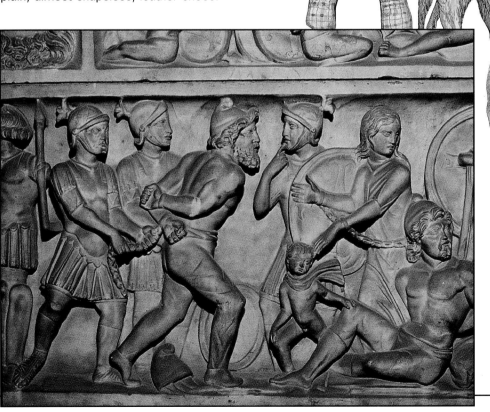

△ **A British woman using a wooden comb.** Her mirror is made of bronze that has been polished so hard that she can see her face reflected in it.

◁ **Carving on a tomb** showing Roman soldiers (in uniform) taking away 'barbarians' in chains. The captives are clothed only around the waist.

ROMAN INFLUENCE

When the Romans took over Britain, they brought with them the Roman way of life – language, food, house styles and dress. These were instantly recognizable as different from British ways.

Roman men had short hair and were clean shaven; British men were long-haired and had beards and moustaches. Also, most Roman clothes were of linen (made from the flax plant) or finely spun wool. These materials are naturally coloured white or cream. Dyed cloth was for special occasions. Roman women did spin and weave cloth. But they also bought cloth that had been made overseas and sold in markets in Britain.

△ **Wealthy Roman men** wore loose linen or woollen robes known as togas. Underneath they wore a tunic. Most British men continued to wear tunics and trousers in coloured checks that looked like today's Scottish tartan.

◁ **A man and woman** dressed for their marriage ceremony – from a relief on a Roman sarcophagus of AD 200.

▷ **Roman clothes had simple designs, too.** Being light in colour, they were hard to keep clean. The Romans soaked them in urine (which is slightly acidic) to get out the stains! The damp British weather drove the Romans to invent a type of raincoat made of oiled wool or animal skin.

◁ **Ist-century AD statuette of a Roman consul** (a very powerful Roman official) dressed in a toga. Later, togas were worn only by important people for ceremonies. Some Roman women wore the equivalent of a toga, called a palla.

△ **Women's clothes were loose-fitting.** They wore underclothes then a long tunic dress. Dresses were made of linen for summer wear and warmer wool for the winter. To go outdoors, women wore a cloak that covered the head.

△ **The emperor wore a purple tunic** or cloak. The dye to make cloth purple was expensive.

Most Roman women spent more time than British women making themselves look neat and tidy. This was because they had servants to run the home and help them dress. They wore simple clothes, but had elaborate hairstyles and jewellery. They also wore make-up. A Roman poet, Martial, complained to his wife, "You live at home, Galla, but your beauty does not. That lives at the chemist's. Your hair was made in faraway Germany, and your teeth are put away in boxes, like your dresses. Even your face sleeps somewhere else."

◁ **The poorest Roman citizens went barefoot.** Most Romans wore leather shoes with metal studs underneath to stop them wearing out. In summer, they wore sandals. Romans kept their hair neat and tidy, and those men and women that could afford it wore jewellery that included rings and bracelets.

DRESSED FOR BATTLE

Throughout Roman and Saxon times, much of Britain was ruled by rival tribes. They fought among themselves or battled with invaders for land and food and to protect their homes and families. Men were always dressed and armed ready to fight.

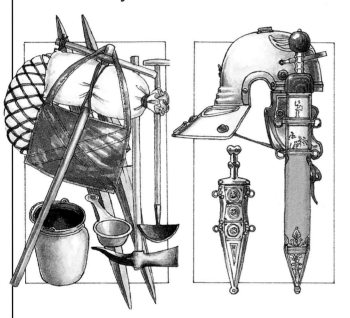

◁ **A Roman soldier's kit** weighed about as much as you weigh! In the leather bag tied to his pole (far left) were clothes, food dishes, a cooking pot, rations (food supplies) and digging tools. He wore a helmet to protect his head, and carried a sword and dagger to fight with (left).

The Romans were able to conquer and keep control of territories because their soldiers were better organized, trained and equipped than their enemies. Roman soldiers had many weapons and wore armour that protected the body well, yet was lightweight enough to allow them to march and fight easily.

The armour covered the top half of the body and the shoulders. It was made of metal plates linked together by leather strips underneath. Beneath the armour, a soldier wore a red woollen tunic, linen underwear and red woollen trousers.

▷ **A Roman soldier ready to march.** His shield is made from wooden strips covered in leather, with metal cross-pieces and a circular boss in the centre to deflect blows.

▷ **Full-time Viking warriors** (about AD 850-900) had chain mail tunics, metal helmets, leather shields, axes, swords and spears. Most part-time Viking raiders had only padded jackets and leather caps as protection. Vikings usually had long hair, beards and moustaches. They often twisted and tied their hair in plaits.

◁ **Anglo-Saxon kings** wearing crowns, with their ministers (right), guards (left) and a captive.

▽ **Saxon warriors** (about AD 450-850) dressed for battle wearing chain mail over ordinary clothes. Those who could afford them had a helmet that covered most of the face and the ears, too.

◁ **Saxon and Viking warriors** had no protection against the cold, damp British climate apart from a cloak and perhaps overtrousers.

As the Roman empire crumbled (in about AD 400), its army in Britain weakened and was slowly withdrawn. It was soon overcome by Anglo-Saxon warriors, who fought more in loose bands and as individuals. They wore their ordinary clothes, covered by lightweight chain mail tunics of various designs. In turn, the Anglo-Saxons were overcome by Viking warriors, who had better weapons and armour.

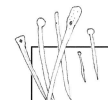

GROWING DIFFERENCES

By Anglo-Saxon times, what people wore was closely linked to how important a person was. Also, people with special jobs, like monks and other Christian priests, dressed differently from ordinary people.

△ **You can tell who these Saxons are by the way they are dressed.**
• The farmers and their wives wear simple wool clothes in plain colours.
• The Christian monks and their helper wear robes and tunics.
• The Saxon lord wears trousers as well as a tunic. These are made from fine wool, dyed deep, rich colours, and are finely decorated.

Nobles and wealthy landowners could afford embroidered cloth, silver brooches and jewellery, and linen underclothes, which were not as rough as wool and did not make the skin itch as much. Ordinary people continued to wear simple clothes.

Men often fastened cloth strips around the bottoms of their trousers. They were joined to their shoes with leather cross-straps. Their shoes did not have heels.

▷ **Anglo-Saxon boots and shoes** were made from leather. Shoes and belts were now made from tanned hide and were more often bought than home-made. Combs and dress pins (far right) were made from wood or bone.

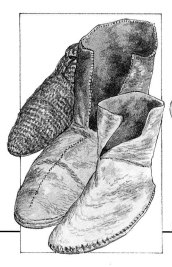 

△ **Anglo-Saxon children were dressed** in clothes like those of their parents. For the first year or so, babies were swaddled (wrapped in linen strips like an Egyptian mummy).

Really rich people could afford to buy cloth that had been made in other countries. Silk, from Asia, was the most expensive of these fabrics, and the most beautiful. Silk can be woven finely and is especially lightweight. It is also very soft. It was used to make tunics, scarfs and dresses. The way silk was dyed in Anglo-Saxon times helped it to keep its colour longer than linen or wool.

◁ **Rich Anglo-Saxons** wore finely decorated clothes. Their cloaks were fixed with sturdy decorative brooches. The soldier shown right wears his cloak fastened at the shoulder so he can get his sword out easily and quickly.

△ **Women weaving woollen cloth.** Clothes were still fairly shapeless. They were held together with belts and pins. In Anglo-Saxon times it became common for women to cover their heads as a sign of modesty.

▷ **Viking ornaments for a woman's dress** – three brooches and beads of coloured glass.

FROM SAXON TO NORMAN

Saxon people were most concerned with wearing clothes that were practical to work and fight in. The Norman conquest in 1066 changed the way people thought about clothes. British dress became increasingly influenced by foreign styles.

∇ **An Anglo-Saxon king with his councillors and bodyguards.** The churchmen wear decorated silk tunics made in France.

The Norman kings gradually made England in to one country. People spent less time fighting. The country got richer, and there was more national and international trade. The wealthy and important people at the royal court had more time to think about manners and dress. They dressed to impress the king.

△ **Men who worked the land** still wore loose-fitting clothes in dark colours that did not show the dirt easily. People mostly kept their hair long.

△ **The Bayeux Tapestry,** which shows the story of the Norman conquest, is our best evidence of clothes and costume in Anglo-Saxon and early Norman times.

△ **A Norman haircut.** The hair is cut short and the back of the head is shaved up to the level of the ears. Sometimes, the top of the head was shaved instead.

△ **A Norman Bible illustration** showing men and women in typical Norman clothing.

◁ **A local lord in the main hall of his castle.** His knights wear chain mail coats, his lords wear long silk tunics. The monk wears a simple brown woollen robe and the houseboy is dressed in a simple tunic and trousers.

This scene from the tapestry shows Normans at a banquet. They are all wearing simple woven tunics and leather shoes. They have short hairstyles.

Clothes were also a way of showing off wealth. Expensive garments were cut, pinned and laced to fit the body more exactly. Instead of thick woollen clothes, people wore several layers of thin cloth, starting with linen underclothes. The robes they wore on top were made of the richest, most decorated cloth. Sleeves became far wider, and less practical.

By the 1200s, the fashion for long, stuffed shoes that stuck out far from the toes had reached a new extreme. The ends of the shoes had to be fastened to the knee to hold them up, otherwise the wearer would trip over them!

Before late-Norman times, wealthy people had worn better clothes in the same style as ordinary people. Now they had better clothes in fancier styles.

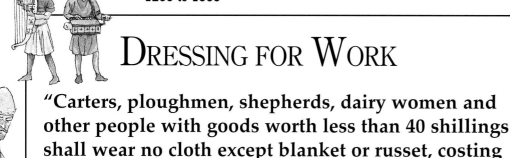

DRESSING FOR WORK

"Carters, ploughmen, shepherds, dairy women and other people with goods worth less than 40 shillings shall wear no cloth except blanket or russet, costing no more than 12 pence a yard."

▽ **Pilgrims journey to Canterbury.** They wear long tunics with hoods.

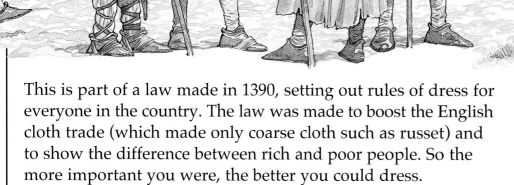

This is part of a law made in 1390, setting out rules of dress for everyone in the country. The law was made to boost the English cloth trade (which made only coarse cloth such as russet) and to show the difference between rich and poor people. So the more important you were, the better you could dress.

△ **Travel was a dirty and difficult business.** People rarely travelled in their best clothes as the dirt roads were either dusty or muddy.

◁ **People made their own cloth less and less.** Many people had jobs in the clothing industry. On the far left, tanners are making leather. Leather was used for shoes, boots and belts. Embroiderers (left) decorated the more expensive cloths with coloured silks or even threads of gold.

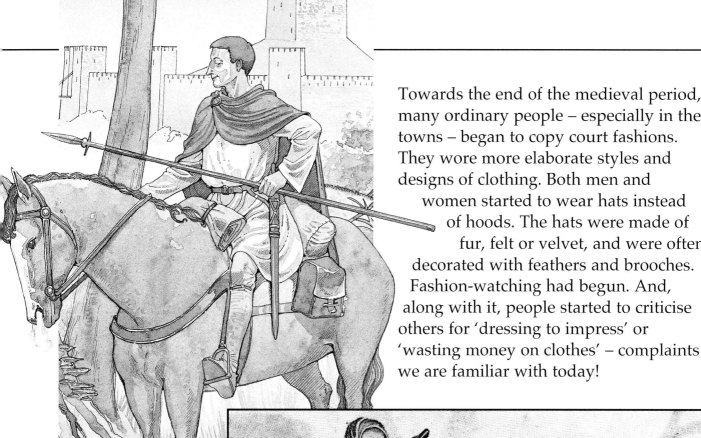

Towards the end of the medieval period, many ordinary people – especially in the towns – began to copy court fashions. They wore more elaborate styles and designs of clothing. Both men and women started to wear hats instead of hoods. The hats were made of fur, felt or velvet, and were often decorated with feathers and brooches. Fashion-watching had begun. And, along with it, people started to criticise others for 'dressing to impress' or 'wasting money on clothes' – complaints we are familiar with today!

△ **A lord returns from a stag hunt.** When not at the royal court, even rich people dressed simply like this.

▷ **Poor people still wore clothes** that were loose and layered, and fastened with belts. This woman wears an apron over her robe.

▷ **Entertainers** wore bright clothes in stripes and patches to catch the eye. Here, a rich couple in fur-edged silk clothes and a poor couple in home-spun, home-dyed wool, listen to a street musician.

◁ **Monks wore habits** and shaved the tops of their heads.

SUITS OF ARMOUR

A law was passed in 1285 declaring: "Every man between fifteen and forty years of age shall provide himself with armour in case he is called to fight. What he provides shall be according to his wealth. Constables will visit each house to check."

The poorest English soldiers went into battle with little more than a helmet, a dagger and a strong leather jacket, maybe reinforced with metal studs. But they used as much armour as they could get – often stealing armour and weapons from bodies on the battlefield.

While soldiers fought on foot, the king and his lords rode into battle on horseback. They wore suits of armour. They were covered from head to toe in chain mail and suits of iron plates. While this gave them better protection, it slowed down their movements.

△ **Welsh archers** wore protective padded tunics. They made their own bows and arrows.

△ **Scottish soldiers,** fighting against the English, made up for their lack of armour by their fierce bravery.

▽ **An army on the march.** Soldiers did not have uniforms. A wealthy lord might provide his soldiers with shields and tunics that were decorated with his family's coat-of-arms. The soldiers might also carry some spare clothing in a backpack.

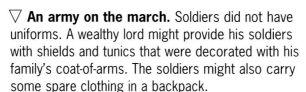

16

Armour was made by smiths. Each suit was individually made-to-measure; there were no factories to produce them. Sheets of iron were beaten into shape using a hammer and anvil. A full suit consisted of a breastplate, backplate, skirt and leg- and arm-guards held together by leather straps and buckles.

Chain mail was made by linking together thousands of small iron rings. The ends of each ring were flattened, pierced and linked by a rivet.

◁ **A knight in shining armour** (far left) gives allegiance to his king on a medieval battlefield. About this time, cannons started to be used in battle. Armour was useless against cannons (centre left) and soon ceased to be used in battle.

▽ **A full suit of armour** might take an hour to put on. By around AD 1500, rivets, not straps and buckles, were used to hold small pieces of armour together. This allowed the wearer greater freedom of movement.

FIT FOR ROYALTY

A courtier described Henry VIII in 1539: "The king wore purple silk, embroidered heavily all over with gold thread. The sleeves were slashed, lined with gold silk, and fastened with buttons of diamonds and pearls. His sword, hat and belt were jewelled, too."

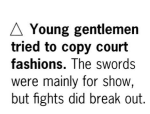

 ▽ **Henry VIII and Queen Anne Boleyn.** The king is wearing padded breeches. These cover his hips and legs as far as the knees.

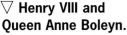

△ **Jane Seymour** (left) **and Anne of Cleves,** Henry VIII's third and fourth wives, wearing jewelled head pieces.

△ **Young gentlemen tried to copy court fashions.** The swords were mainly for show, but fights did break out.

Fashions reached new heights in the Tudor courts. Styles of clothing changed rapidly. Noblemen began wearing breeches instead of hose. At first these were puffed and short, then they were made slender. Womens' necklines were low then high. People wore more layers of clothing. There were even layers of sleeves, the top set partly 'slashed' to show some of the cloth underneath.

Expensive fabrics like silk and velvet were made even more luxurious with jewels or fine embroidery in coloured thread, even gold. Conspicuous dressing – in order to stand out in a crowd – was 'the in thing'.

▽ **Elizabethan ladies took a long time to dress.** They had lots of layers of clothes, padding and stiffening to be buttoned, hooked or tied into place. They could never have got into it all without the help of a maid.

△ **Elizabeth I in Parliament.** She is wearing her crown, royal gown and robe. Her advisors stand on either side of her. They are dressed in their finest robes and ruff collars. Before her sit ministers and leading churchmen. The churchmen are wearing skull caps.

◁ **A portrait of Edward VI,** showing him as a young man. He is wearing a lace shirt with cuffs, a beautifully embroidered buttoned jacket, and a silk robe with fur collar. His feathered cap, too, is edged with fur.

Tudor courtiers used various aids to make their bodies look more attractive. Stomachers were pieces of bone, shaped like a long thin oval, which flattened a lady's stomach and pushed up her chest. A padded roll around the waist made skirts stand out nicely all around. Men put padding down their stockings to make their calves look fatter and well-muscled, and they put codpieces in their breeches to exaggerate their 'manhood'!

TUDOR WORKING CLOTHES

Uniforms – similar clothes worn by people doing the same kinds of jobs – became more common in Tudor times. The designs of hats, dresses, jackets, jerkins and footwear changed as people's jobs became more varied and specialized.

Butchers, bakers, blacksmiths and cooks put on aprons to prevent their clothing getting dirty. They also wore caps to keep their long hair out of the way. New professional men, such as magistrates, JPs and town clerks, wore doublets, breeches, gowns and usually a flat cap. Outdoor workers usually wore tall felt hats and loose-fitting tunics and breeches.

▽ **Dressed for work.** Left to right are: a merchant (wearing a ruff), a shepherd, a nightwatchman (wearing a felt hat) and the merchant's daughter. These are followed by a farmworker, the merchant's son, the farmer's wife (on a horse) and a sailor.

▽ **Old pictures** can tell us a lot about clothes, but they were painted to look attractive, like this one for King Edward IV. Miners at the time would not really have dressed so well!

▷ **In a Tudor tailor's workshop.** The tailor is cutting the cloth while his apprentice sews together the pieces. Finished garments hang from hooks on the wall – breeches, hats and capes. A pair of stockings are draped over a pipe. Most tailors' shops were small and were run from the front ground-floor room of the Tudor house.

△ **The weaver** folds up her sleeves so they do not catch in the loom. Her close-fitting cap keeps her hair tidy.

△ **The butcher** wears a leather apron to keep his clothes clean. He is also wearing a ruff – he is a follower of fashion.

△ **The baker** (above left) wears a simple linen shift and breeches. The nightwatchman (above) and sailors (left and below) wear long padded breeches and leather or thick cloth doublets to keep warm and dry.

Men mostly wore underwear, shirts, doublets (jackets with removable sleeves) and breeches. In early Tudor times, they wore cloth stockings fastened to the breeches. Later, these stockings were made from wool or knitted silk.

When Elizabeth I was queen, ruffs were in fashion. Ruffs were starched and folded hoops of cloth worn around the neck. They began small, but got so big that the wearers had to eat with long-handled spoons!

FASHION FOR ALL

The Stuart period saw an explosion of extreme fashions, especially after King Charles II came to the throne in 1660. In the Georgian period that followed, new inventions made cloth cheaper and helped fashion reach ordinary people more than ever before.

▷ **Stuart courtiers, lords and ladies** wore the height of fashion. Their clothes were made of brightly coloured silks and linens, and were often decorated with ribbon loops, bows and clusters, and with lace neckcloths. Men and women wore carefully shaped leather, make-up and jewellery.

▽ **One of the king's cavalrymen and a Parliamentary foot-soldier.** What you wore often told people who you supported in the English Civil War. Supporters of the king dressed the most extravagantly.

△ **How people dressed told you about their religion, too.** Many Protestant Christian groups (like the Puritans shown here) believed people should dress simply, not vainly, in sombre colours.

▽ **'Costume of nobility and gentry'** – an illustration from about 1690. The men are wearing wigs and high-heeled shoes, the ladies head-dresses and gowns. The lady on the right has a muff to keep her hands warm.

From the late Stuart period, trade increased greatly and the country got richer. Markets were soon full of exciting things from abroad, including cloth.

From America came a new kind of cloth, cotton, which could be spun very fine. Machines were invented which spun wool, silk and cotton finely and quickly. Machines could now do the weaving, too. This made all cloth cheaper, and more widely available. Now there were very few people who still made their own clothes, and even fewer who made their own cloth.

△ **Wealthy Georgians in their fine daily wear.** Notice how the child is dressed exactly like her mother, in a long gown.

▽ **By Georgian times, everyone was wearing the fashions of the day,** like the wealthy landowners below.

Rich people wore expensive clothes and a lot of make up, including fake beauty spots called patches. They also wore wigs, which they powdered. At parties, they competed to have the most extravagant wigs – some women had flowers, feathers, even caged birds, built into them! Both men and women also wore high-heeled shoes – with real jewels on for parties!

△ **From left to right:** a factory owner in a suit; working class children; a squire wearing a frock coat, felt hat and leather boots; a country lad, milkmaid, farm worker and chimney sweep all in working clothes; a lord's grooms; a gentleman, his wife and daughter.

◁ **Soldiers and sailors** (ship's crew, left) now had uniforms to wear.

23

PRIM AND PROPER

Queen Victoria was not fashion-conscious. She was more concerned with her family than with the court, and lived and dressed relatively simply.

As queen, Victoria set an example for modest dressing, etiquette and formality. Her ministers and advisors would always wear sombre suits, and take off their top hats and gloves in her presence. The staff of her household were always smart and neatly dressed.

▽ **Queen Victoria's coronation.** She wore a simple white dress that hung off her shoulders. Like most women at the time, she wore her hair parted in the centre and pulled back into a bun.

▷ **Princess Victoria and her governess** ride in a carriage. Both ladies are wearing long gloves, a bonnet with ribbons, and have their hair long, fashioned into ringlets at the sides. The princess wears a neat dress.

△ **"Poverty and Wealth"** – a famous painting of the 1840s by artist William Frith. You can compare the costume and clothes of rich and poor people. One of the poor girls has no shoes.

However, some people in Victorian times were still interested in fashion. But now, instead of imitating the court, they looked to other countries, especially to France, for ideas. More people could read, so sales of ladies' magazines (which were first published in Georgian times) boomed. They had not only pictures and descriptions of all the latest fashions but also paper patterns for making them.

△ **Officers of the Scots Guards** – a photograph from about 1900. The decoration on their jackets and caps are legacies from the fashionable Georgian period.

▷ **Soldiers from various regiments of the army about 1855.** Their decorative uniforms, with brass buttons, braiding, shoulder straps and high collars, made their lives all the harder. Thanks to the new chemical dyes, the coats, especially the red ones, were very bright. It made soldiers look smart but also made them easier targets for the enemy.

▽ **Queen Victoria in 1887 celebrating fifty years of her rule.** After her husband, Prince Albert, died (in 1861), Victoria never wore anything but black, the colour of mourning.

At the beginning of the Victorian period, chemical dyes were invented. Suddenly it was possible to dye cloth in very bright or very deep colours. For a while, dress shops sold only clothes in a riot of colours, tartans and stripes. Then, as everyone became able to afford this sort of cloth, the fashion swung back towards more delicate colours!

VICTORIAN WORKERS

"The workers of Manchester wear mainly cotton, not wool or linen (which would wear out less)," an observer wrote in 1844. "Women wear dresses, men trousers and jackets of fustian, a heavy cotton."

Throughout the Victorian period, clothes were shaped to fit the body. Rich, ordinary and poor people still wore different sorts of clothes, even though there were no longer laws about clothing. Everyone wore hats or caps.

▽ **A businessman** wears a raincoat and top hat, his wife and children bonnets and capes. The working class children are dressed in tattered clothing.

▽ **Men wore trousers that ended at the knee** (left). Working class girls wore smocks over their dresses to keep them clean.

△ **A doctor and his well-dressed family**. It was still traditional for children to be dressed in simpler versions of adult clothes.

▽ **'The Railway Station'** – painted by William Frith in 1862. The women wear crinolines (frames under the skirts to hold them clear of the legs). The men are dressed in dark-coloured suits and hats.

△ **Chimney sweeps and child miners** mostly worked barefoot and wore 'rags', which they threw away once they got too dirty to scrub clean.

▽ **Farm workers at harvest time** wore wide-brimmed hats and long smocks, to avoid getting sunburnt and to protect them from scratchy stalks. Men had their hair cut short, ladies had longer hair tied up in buns or curls.

▷ **Two maids and the cook from a doctor's house.** Servants were supposed to dress neatly at all times. Maids had to wear a cap and apron when out of the kitchen. This made them look 'smart' and underlined the fact that they were servants.

△ **A Victorian family on a day out by the seaside.** Notice how well everyone is dressed. Had their clothes got dirty on the trip, they would have been given to the servants to wash and iron.

▷ **These building workers** wear fustian (heavy cotton) jackets, trousers and waistcoats. Their shirts are a lighter cotton and have no collar. Collars, which got dirty quickly, were bought separately and buttoned on. They were regularly washed and starched.

Poor people could not follow fashion. As always, they dressed in whatever they could make or buy from second-hand shops. Henry Mayhew, who wrote a book about the London poor, described the children: "They wear whatever rags they can scavenge, for as long as they hold, or can be pinned or tied together. When they fall off the body, then is the time to scavenge more."

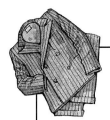

TWENTIETH-CENTURY FASHION

With wealth from industry and trade, and with new technology, everyday life has changed rapidly since 1901. Fashion has been no exception. It has seen great changes, most of them labelled 'shocking'.

Synthetic fabrics (made from chemicals not natural fibres) and automated machinery to spin and weave fabrics made good-quality, attractive clothing available to all. The home sewing machine led to people buying dress patterns and fabric and once again making their own clothes. They could make fashionable clothes more cheaply than they could buy them in shops. Zips changed the way clothes were fastened, providing a quick, close-fitting alternative to buttons.

▷ **Fashion took off again in the 1910s.** This woman's clothes were fashioned in France.

▽ **A Second World War soldier.** Uniforms were made tougher and in drab colours for better camouflage.

▷ **US soldiers and airmen dancing with English girls** in 1945. Most of the women have curled their hair.

◁ **1950s fashion.** For the first time, young children wore different sorts of clothes from adults. Girls wore dresses and boys wore shorts until they were about eleven years old, when they changed to long trousers. Most shoes were still made from leather. But many of the clothes were made from synthetic fabrics such as nylon, rayon and polyester.

△ **Clothes from the 1960s.** Most women wore a 'mini' (very short) skirt, or at least a skirt above the knee. People wore shoes made from plastic and other synthetic materials. Some clothes designers even made paper, plastic and metal clothes!

△ **In the1970s** almost everyone had a pair of flared jeans (denim trousers that got wider below the knees). Many men and women grew their hair long. 'Unisex' clothes and hairstyles (for men or women) became popular. Teenagers wore thick-soled 'platform' shoes.

In the 1990s fashion has changed again. Fewer people make their own clothes. They tend to buy a wide range of clothes and to dress more casually, even for work. Some youngsters dress in clothes that their parents find 'scruffy'. As fashions are revived, many people buy clothes in second-hand shops that make money for charities. What will the next century bring to clothes and costume?

◁ **In the 1950s fashion had a new target – the teenagers.** They dressed in ways that showed a new-found freedom and greater spending power.

▽ **1990s models** exhibiting a new range of fashions, influenced by 1960s styles. Designers often look to the past for fresh inspiration.

Places to Visit

All of these places have been suggested because they have either clothing collections, or a significant number of paintings which show clothing from a particular period.

Bath Museum of Costume, Assembly Rooms, Bath.
Bethnal Green Museum of Childhood, Bethnal Green, London.
Castle Howard Costume Galleries, Castle Howard, Malton, Yorkshire.
Costume Museum, Castle Gate, Nottingham.
Devon Collection of Costume, Bogan House, High Street, Totnes, Devon.
Gallery of English Costume, Platt Hall, Platt Fields, Kisholme, Manchester.
Grantham Museum, St. Peter's Hill, Grantham, Lincolnshire.
Hitchin Museum, Hitchin, Hertfordshire.
Ipswich Museum, High Street, Ipswich, Suffolk. Reconstructions, especially good for early clothing (Britons, Romans).
Peterborough City Museum and Art Gallery, Priestgate, Peterborough, Cambridgeshire.
Elizabethan House, Plymouth, Devon.
Geoffreye Museum, London.
Highland Folk Museum, Kingussie, Scotland.
Museum of Costume and Lace, Castle Street, Exeter, Devon.
Museum of London, London Wall, London. Tudor section, including clothes.
Museum of Leathercraft, 60, Bridge Street, Northampton.
National Portrait Gallery, St. Martin's Place, London.
National Trust Collection of Costume, Kilworth House, Broadclyst, Exeter, Devon.
National Museum of Scotland, Chambers Street, Edinburgh, Scotland.
Strangers' Hall, Norwich, Norfolk.
Tate Gallery, Millbank, London.
Victoria and Albert Museum, London.
Welsh Folk Museum, St. Fagin's, Cardiff.
Wygston's Museum of Costume, Applegate, Leicester.

Further Reading

A History of Fashion, J.A. Black and M.A. Garland, Orbis, 1980.
Costume in Detail, 1730–1930, Nancy Bradfield, Harrap, 1968.
Historical Costume of England, 1066–1956, Nancy Bradfield, Harrap, 1958.
Costume in Context: Victorians, Jennifer Ruby, Batsford, 1987.
Costume in Context: Tudors, Jennifer Ruby, Batsford, 1987.
What we Wore, Stuart Ross, Wayland, 1991.
Costume Reference, Vols 1–9 (Romans to 1950), all by M. Sichel, Batsford, 1977.
Everyday Costume in England, A. Barfoot, Batsford, 1961.
Clothes as seen by Four Generations, Ruth Thompson, Watts, 1992.
Tudor and Stuart Clothes, Peter Chrisp, Wayland, 1994.
Victorian Clothes, Lyn Gash, Wayland, 1993.
Everyday Dress 1650 –1900, E. Ewing, Batsford, 1971.

GLOSSARY

apprentice someone who agrees to work with a master for a number of years to learn his trade, like baking.

barbarians people with another way of life to the person calling them barbarian, uncivilized.

boss round, raised metal stud in the centre of a shield.

breeches trousers that reach to about the knee.

chain mail armour made up of lots of metal rings linked together to make a vest or leggings.

civilized well-behaved.

constables people in Elizabethan England who were chosen to enforce the law in the local area.

court the monarch and the people who lived and worked with the monarch.

courtiers the people who lived and worked with the monarch.

dye to make something another colour, usually by soaking it in a coloured liquid.

embroidery sewing patterns onto cloth in a contrasting colour or colours.

habit monks' clothing.

JP Justice of the Peace, a local government official, first set up in Elizabethan times.

merchant someone who sells things made or grown by other people.

monarch a king or queen.

monk a person who, for religious reasons, shuts himself off from the world to pray and follow his religion.

musketeer a soldier who fired a musket, a long, hand-held gun, rather like a rifle, used in the sixteenth and seventeenth centuries.

noble from one of the rich and important families in the country. Nobles usually had a title, like Duke of York.

ornaments decorative objects such as rings, bracelets, brooches and necklaces.

preacher a Christian clergyman or priest.

robe a garment worn by men and women that was like a full-length, long-sleeved tunic.

ruffs frilled collars that stick out round the neck.

spin to twist fibres or hair together to make long strands.

swaddled wrapped tightly in long strips of cloth with arms and legs straight down.

tailor a person who makes clothes.

weave to turn threads into cloth by passing them under and over each other to hold them together.

woad blue dye, made from the woad plant. It was used to dye clothes. The ancient Britons were said to paint themselves with woad.

yard just under a metre in length.

INDEX